Author and Illustrator based on the
Isle of Man

The Magical Rainbow Garden

By Sheila K Clark

Illustrated by Emma West

Copyright Sheila © 2020 K Clark

All rights reserved, no part of this publication may be reproduced, distributed or transmitted in any from means, included photocopying, recording or any other mechanical methods without prior written permission of the publisher.

A CIP catalogue record is available from the British Library.

ISBN: 9798682035854

Meeka Manx Moon

Acknowledgments

I would like to express my special thanks of gratitude to my friends and family who helped and supported me through this book, and a thank you for Emma for the illustrations.

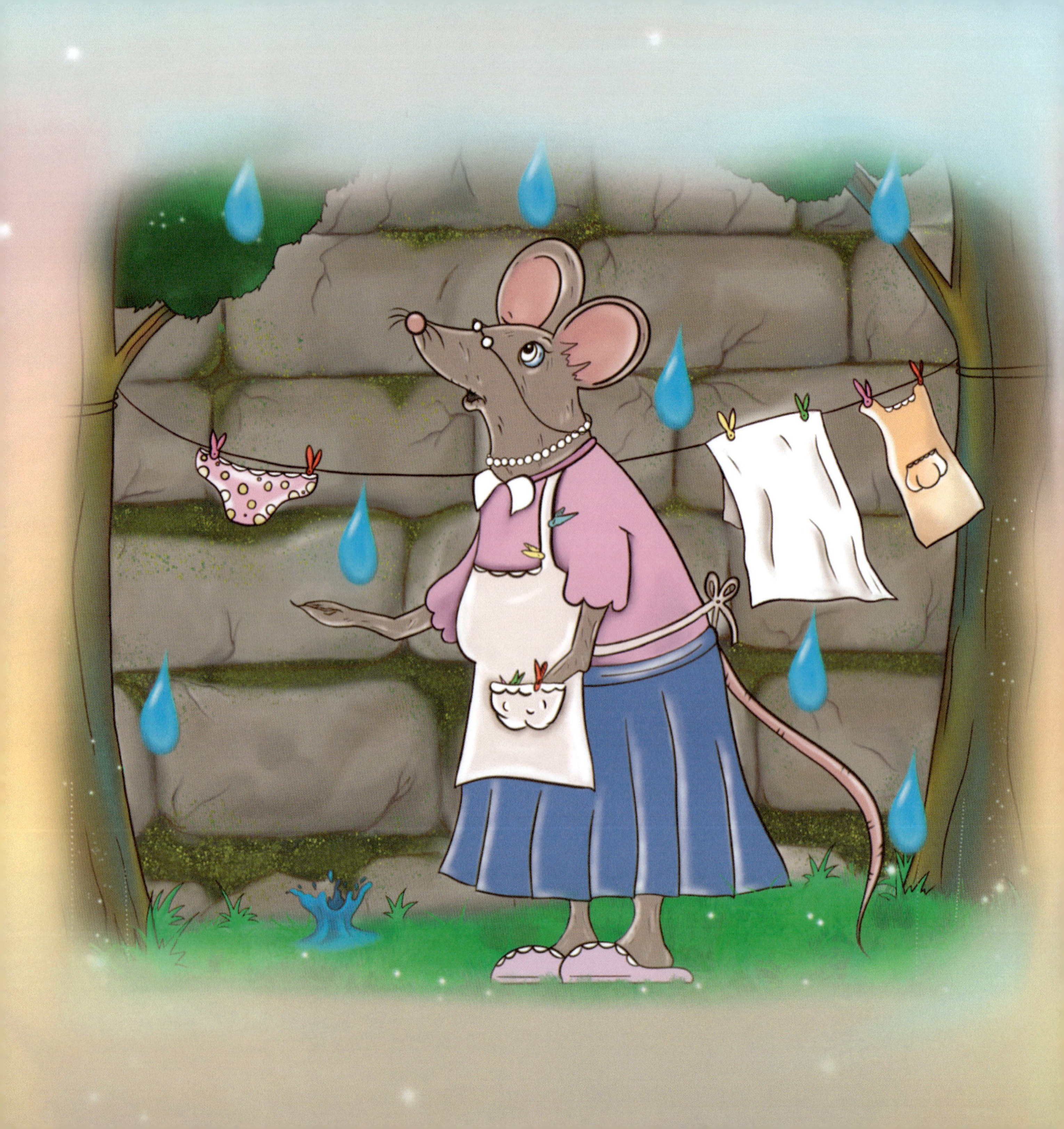

All is well in The Rainbow Garden. The sun is shining, the rainbows are dancing, and everyone is happy, it is a beautiful day.

One of the oldest animals that live in the garden, Miss Quirky the mouse, does the washing for everyone, because she likes to see all the clothes hanging out on her washing line sparkling in the sunshine.

It was early morning and time for Miss Quirky to hang out the washing by the Big Wall, she hangs it here to stop the wind from blowing all the clothes away and being lost forever so Mrs Brown the rabbit doesn't have to make more clothes for everyone.

Suddenly Miss Quirky felt a drop of rain on her head, Mr Brush the hedgehog came over to ask "Have you seen Mrs Brown? I need her to make me an umbrella; it never rains in Rainbow Garden: what is happening?" said Mr Brush.

"I'm not sure, let's go and see The Wise Old Apple Tree; he will know what to do," said Miss Quirky the mouse.

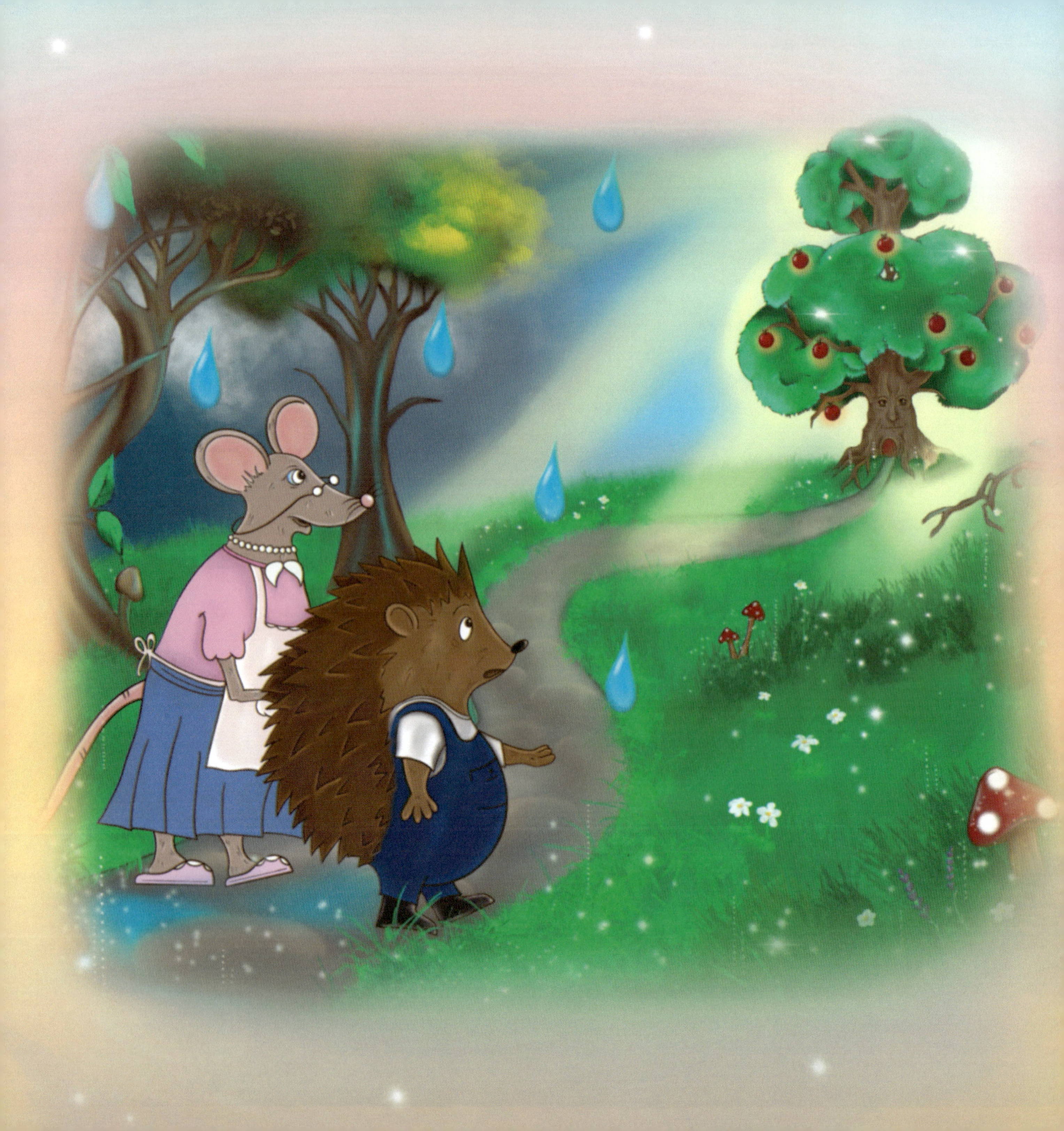

After walking a little way to see The Wise Old Apple Tree, they realised it had stopped raining. "Hooray, I don't need an umbrella now," said Mr Brush. "I can go back to hang out the washing," replied Miss Quirky while smiling.
So off they went back home. However, as they approached the big wall, it started to rain again! "Oh dear we shall definitely have to see The Wise Old Apple Tree now!" exclaimed Miss Quirky.

Suddenly, Miss Longlegs the spider was scurrying towards them, "It's been raining so much that my web has broken, now I can't bathe in the sunshine between the washing line and the Big Wall" cried Miss Longlegs. "Oh dear!" said Mr Brush, "Miss Quirky and I are going to see The Wise Old Apple Tree, he will know what to do, would you like to come with us?" "Yes please!" said Miss Longlegs. So, they set off back towards The Wise Old Apple Tree, but as they continued walking, they heard a croaking sound.

It was Mr Green the frog, who lived in the pond by the Big Wall. He was very agitated, "My pond will overflow" he croaked. "It was raining so hard that I'm afraid our friends The Rainbow Flowers will lose their petals and we will have no rainbows in the garden again, what can we do?" Said Mr Green. "We are off to see The Wise Old Apple Tree, would you like to come with us?" said Miss Quirky the mouse, "he will know what to do".

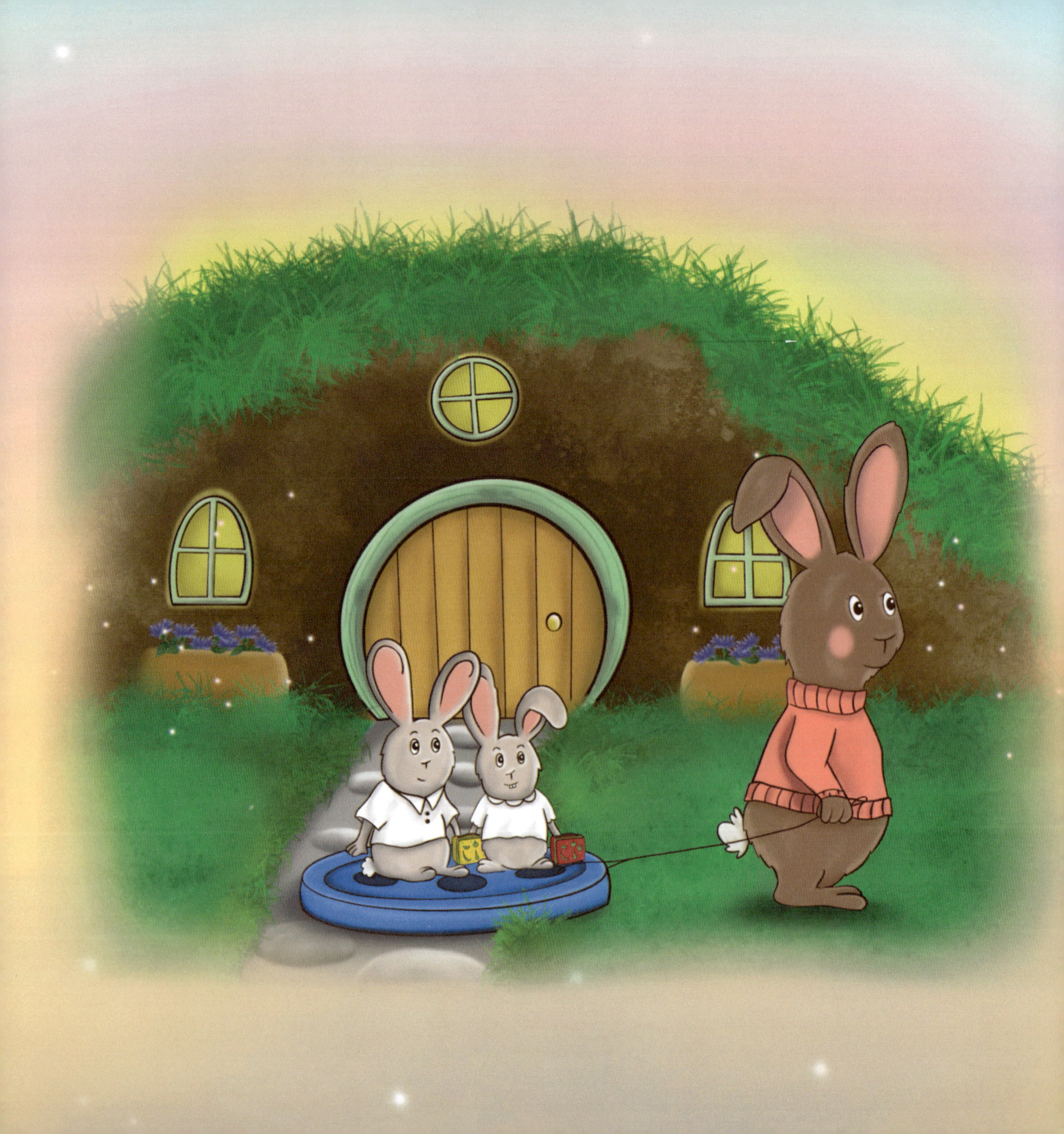

The Wise Old Apple Tree with his shining red apples, was so tall he could be seen over the other side of the garden he could almost touch the sky.
While walking to visit the tree, Mrs Brown the Rabbit popped out of her house on the grassy verge. It appeared she was pulling something out behind her.
Her twins Bounty and Snowball were sitting on a round object that was flat like a wheel.
"What do you have there?" Asked Miss Quirky.
"I don't know," said Mrs Brown, "but it very useful for pulling the twins along, it rolled into our house this morning and gave us such a fright."
"We're all going to go and see The Wise Old Apple Tree do you want to come with us? He will tell you what it is" said Mr Green.
"I would but I have to get the twins to school, can you describe it to him and see if he knows what it could be?" said Mrs Brown.

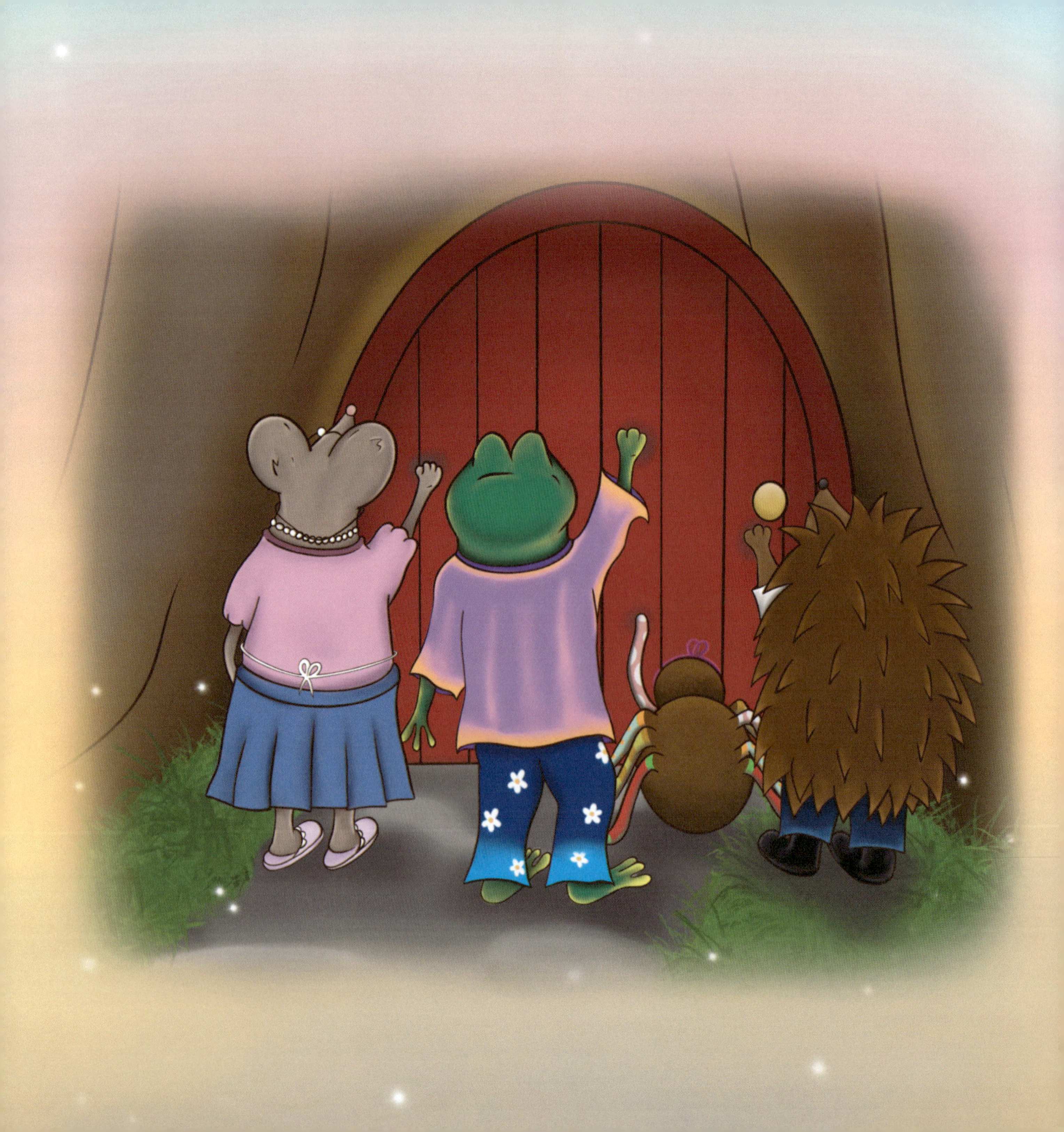

As they got nearer to The Wise Old Apple Tree, Miss Quirky said "Who is going to knock on the door and talk to him?"

"Oh dear" said Miss Longlegs the spider "I'm too shy and I'm afraid I will scurry away."

"Oh dear" said Mr Green the frog "I am so nervous I will keep croaking and lose my voice."

"Oh dear" said Mr Brush the hedgehog "I will curl up into a ball and roll away"

"Then I shall talk to him, but we must all knock on the door together," decided Miss Quirky.

Once they agreed, they approached The Wise Old Apple Tree and knocked on the door.

"Who is making that noise," thundered the deep voice of The Wise Old Apple Tree.

"We need your help sir; you are wise and know everything," said Miss Quirky the Mouse.

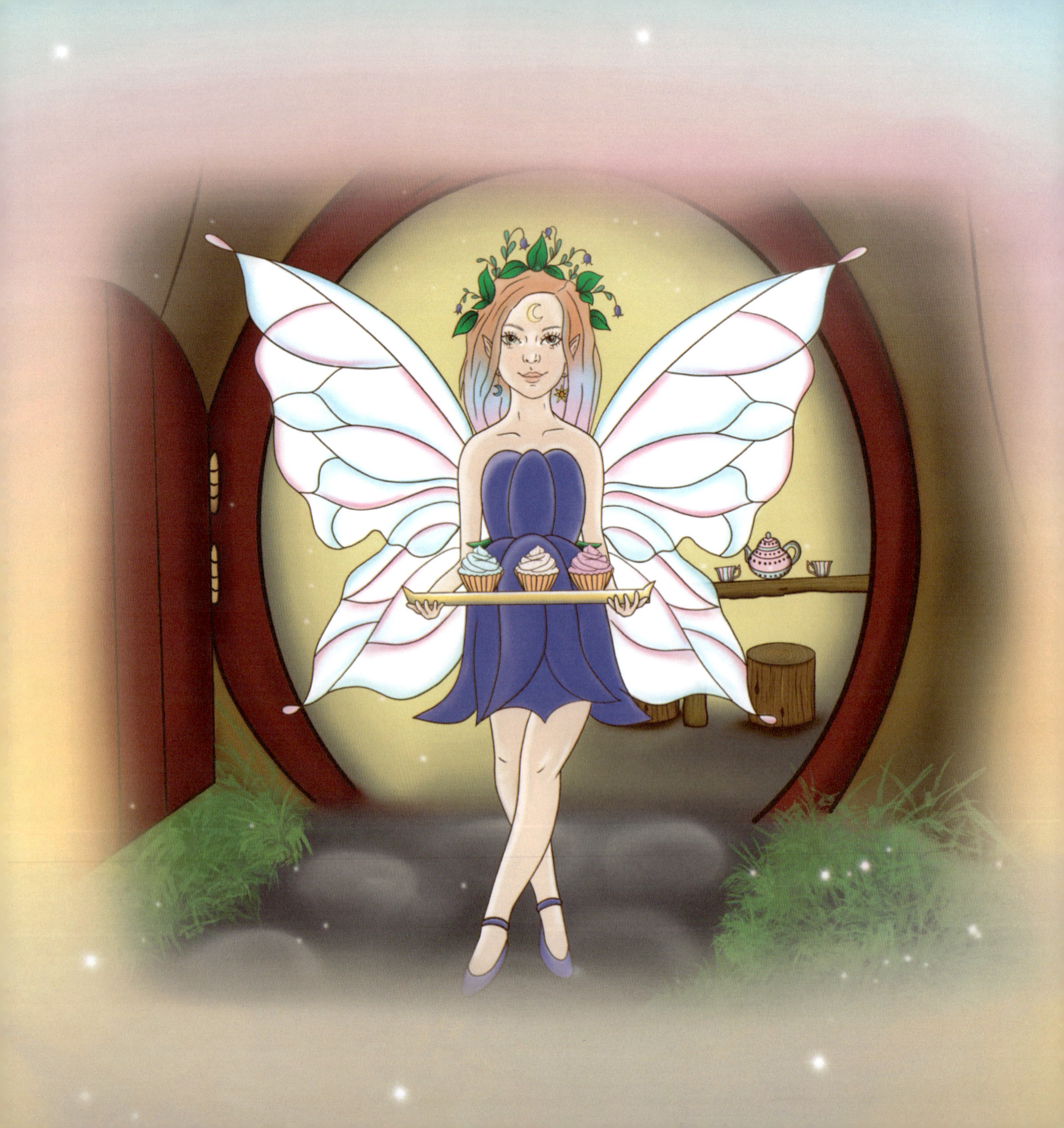

"Of course, what can I help you with?" thundered The Wise Old Apple Tree.
The door opened and Vorriebell the fairy whose dress was like a bluebell opened the door with a tray of cakes.

Miss Quirky told The Wise Old Apple Tree the story about the rain by the Big Wall and about the unusual object that rolled into Mrs Brown the Rabbits house that morning.

"Well now," said The Wise Old Apple Tree, "I will send Hoot the Owl to find out why it is raining by the Big Wall, while we wait you should have some of Vorriebells fairy cakes."
No one in Rainbow Garden would refuse Vorriebells cakes as they were so delicious.

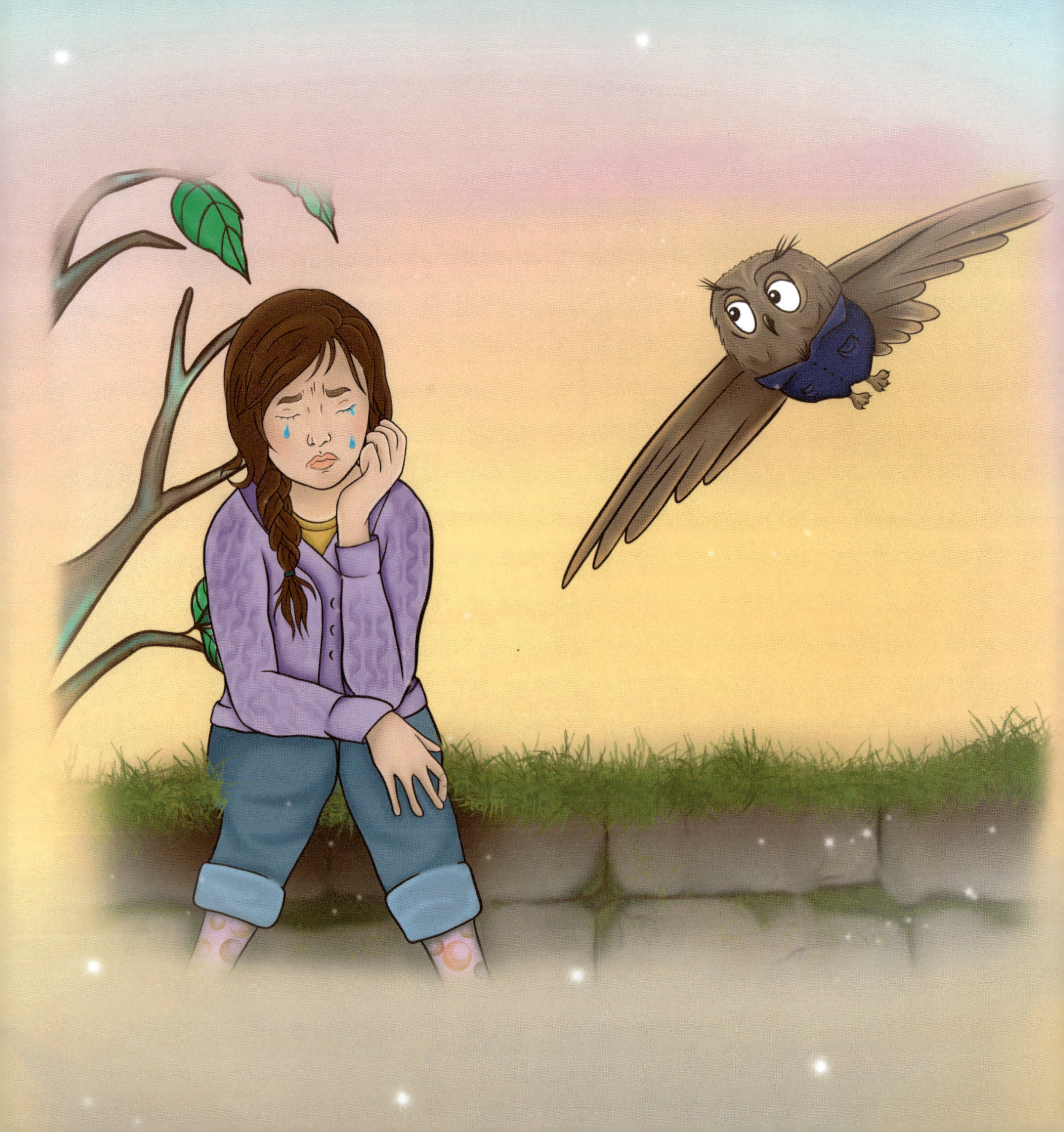

A little while later when Hoot the Owl returned. "Why is it raining beside the Big Wall?" said The Wise Old Apple Tree.
"There is a human girl sitting on the wall crying," said Hoot.
Everyone looked shocked, "We need to do something, our friends the Rainbow Flowers are in danger of losing their petals" cried Hoot. "Yes indeed," said The Wise Old Apple Tree. "Vorriebell can you help?"
"Absolutely" said Vorriebell. "Please go to the Big Wall and use your magic to help her stop crying!" asked The Wise Old Apple Tree.
So off she flew to the Big Wall. The others thanked The Wise Old Apple Tree before they set off home.
"Not to worry your problem will soon be sorted now Vorriebell is helping you!" said the tree.

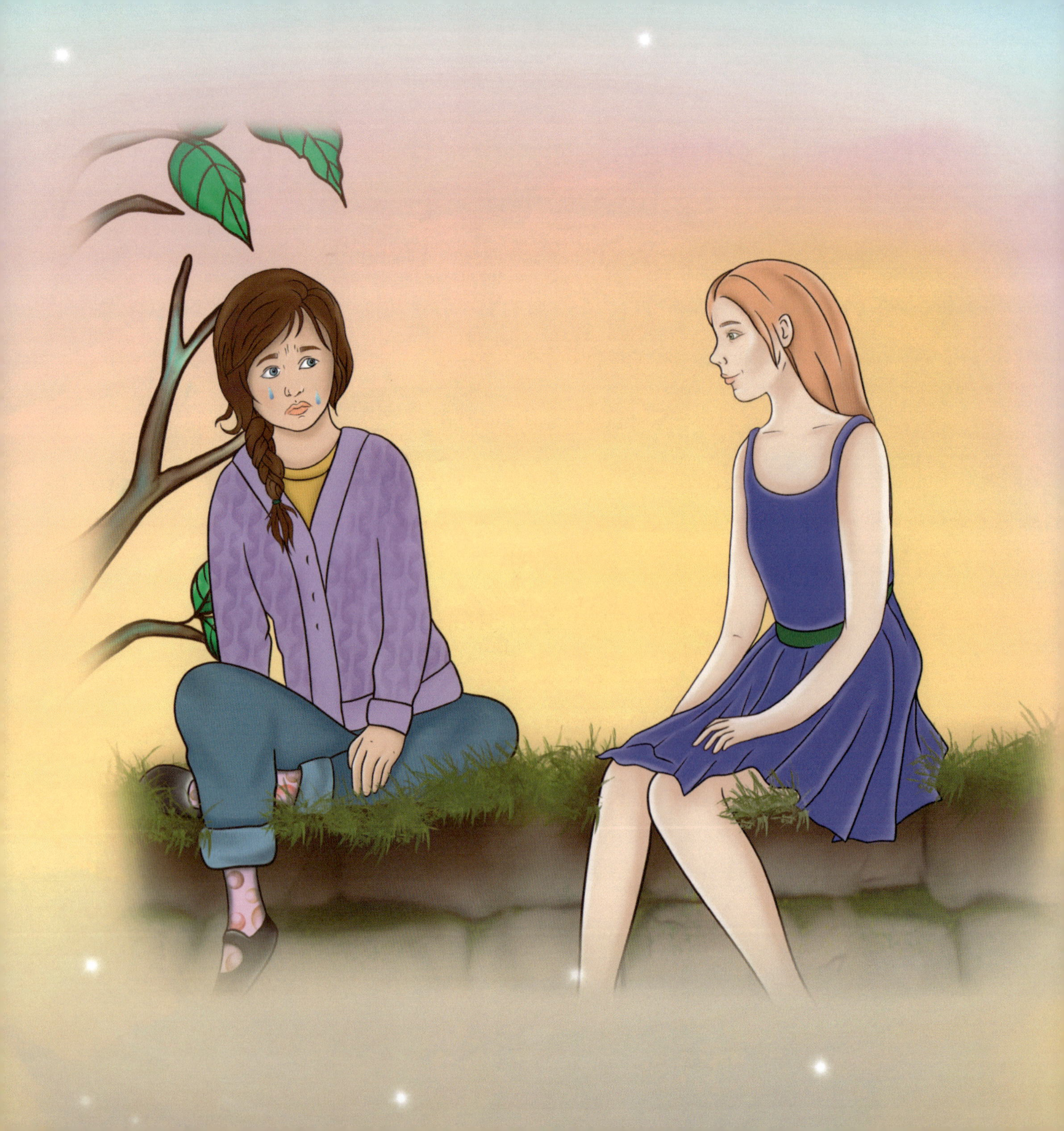

Vorriebell spotted the girl still sitting on the Big Wall and still crying.

Before approaching, Vorriebell used her magic to make herself the same size as the girl and climbed up the Big Wall.

"Are you okay?" Said Vorriebell. "I'm sorry," said the little girl "I didn't notice you sitting there, there's a prize at school today for the best knitted cardigan and I have lost one of my buttons."

"I will help you find your button," Vorriebell replied, she was pleased when she saw the girl smile slightly.

"My name is Vorriebell, what is yours."

"My name is Rowena, thank you for helping me try to find my button!"

Vorriebell told Rowena that she was really a fairy with magic powers and spoke about all the animals in the Rainbow Garden and about The Wise Old Apple Tree.

Starting to whisper, Vorriebell said "You must not tell anyone about my magic powers, but I can make us both smaller, it will be easier to find your button that way," said Vorriebell. "Now Rowena, please shut your eyes and believe," so Rowena shut her eyes and excitedly believed.

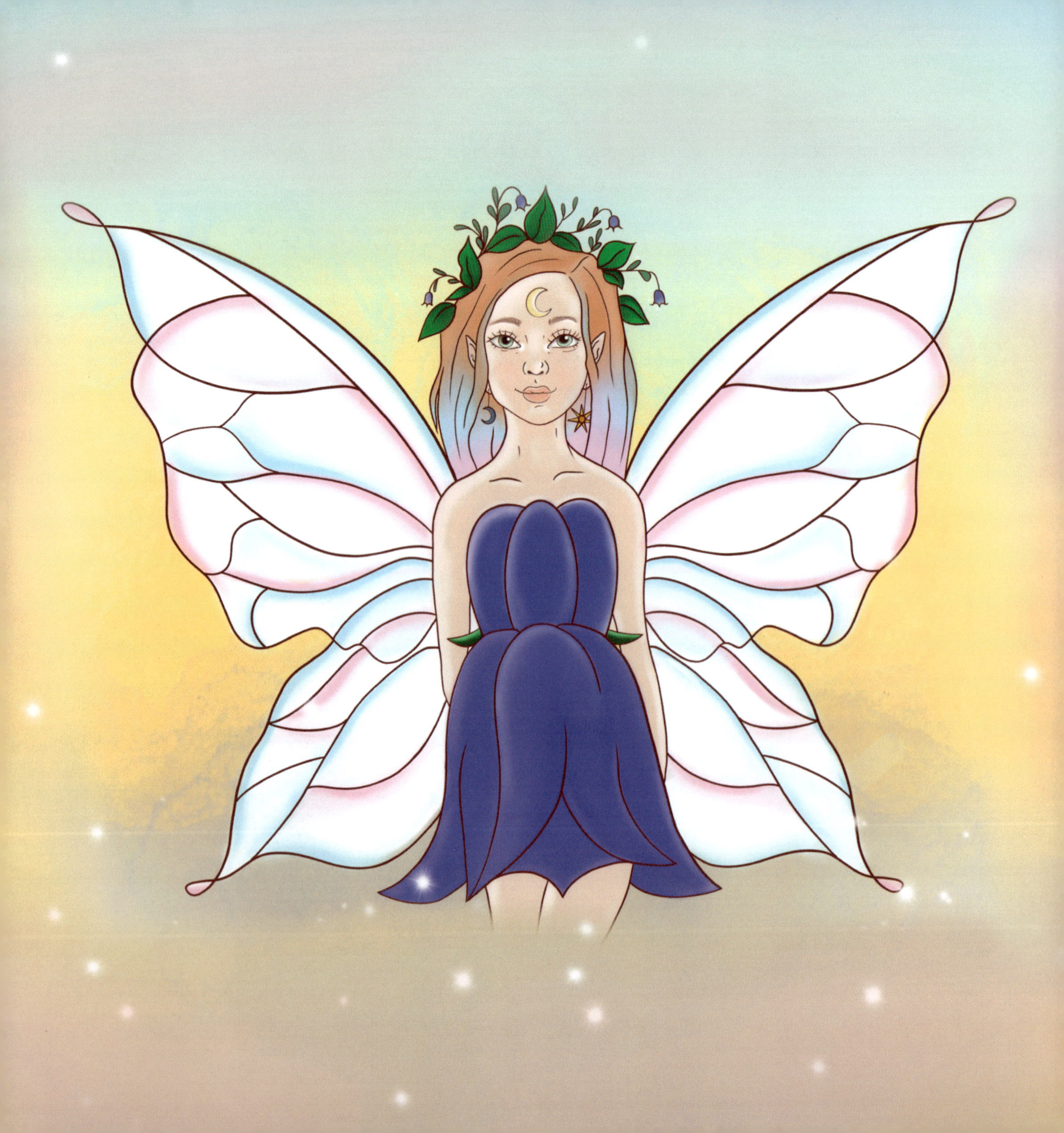

Vorriebell started to work her magic and shouted "Open!" Rowena opened her eyes and she was much smaller than before, she could see Vorriebell with wings, "I can't believe I have met a real fairy!" she said excitedly.

Rowena looked at the rainbow flowers in amazement, "Look at those!" she said. "They make rainbows for us every morning, now you have stopped crying they can make rainbows again."

"I'm so sorry." said Rowena.

"It's okay we forgive you," said all the Rainbow Flowers together.

"Did they just speak? That is wonderful," remarked Rowena with a gleaming smile on her face.

"I think I know where we might find your button, I heard Miss Quirky the mouse telling The Wise Old Apple Tree about a round object rolling into Mrs Brown the rabbits house," said Vorriebell.

Rowena looked surprisingly at Vorriebell and said "Do all the creatures talk? And will I be late for school?"

Vorriebell started to laugh and said "Yes they do! Don't worry you won't be late, there is no time here."

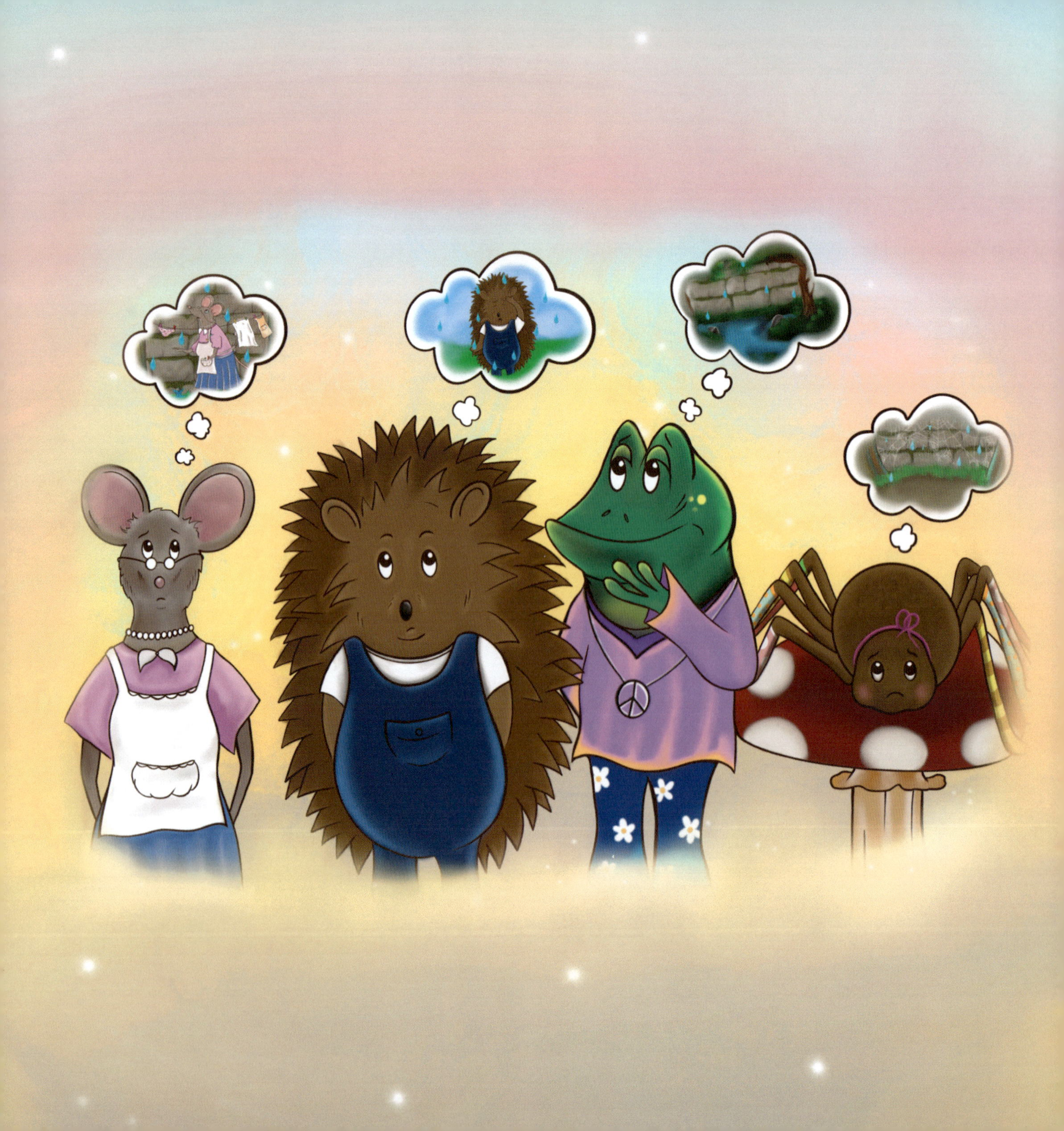

When looking for Rowenas button, the other animals were almost back from The Wise Old Apple Tree and spotted Vorriebell with the girl.
Rowena looked shocked as she had never seen animals wearing clothes before. Vorriebell introduced Rowena to them all and explained to them that she was crying because she lost her button of her cardigan.
"Oh you poor girl," said Miss Quirky "I think Mrs Brown the Rabbit might have your button she was using it to pull her twins around earlier."

The animals told Rowena all about their problems they had poor Miss Quirky was thinking about her washing, Mr Green The Frog was worrying about his pond overflowing, Miss Longlegs couldn't think of anything but bathing in the sunshine.
And as for Mr Brush all that was on his mind was keeping dry.

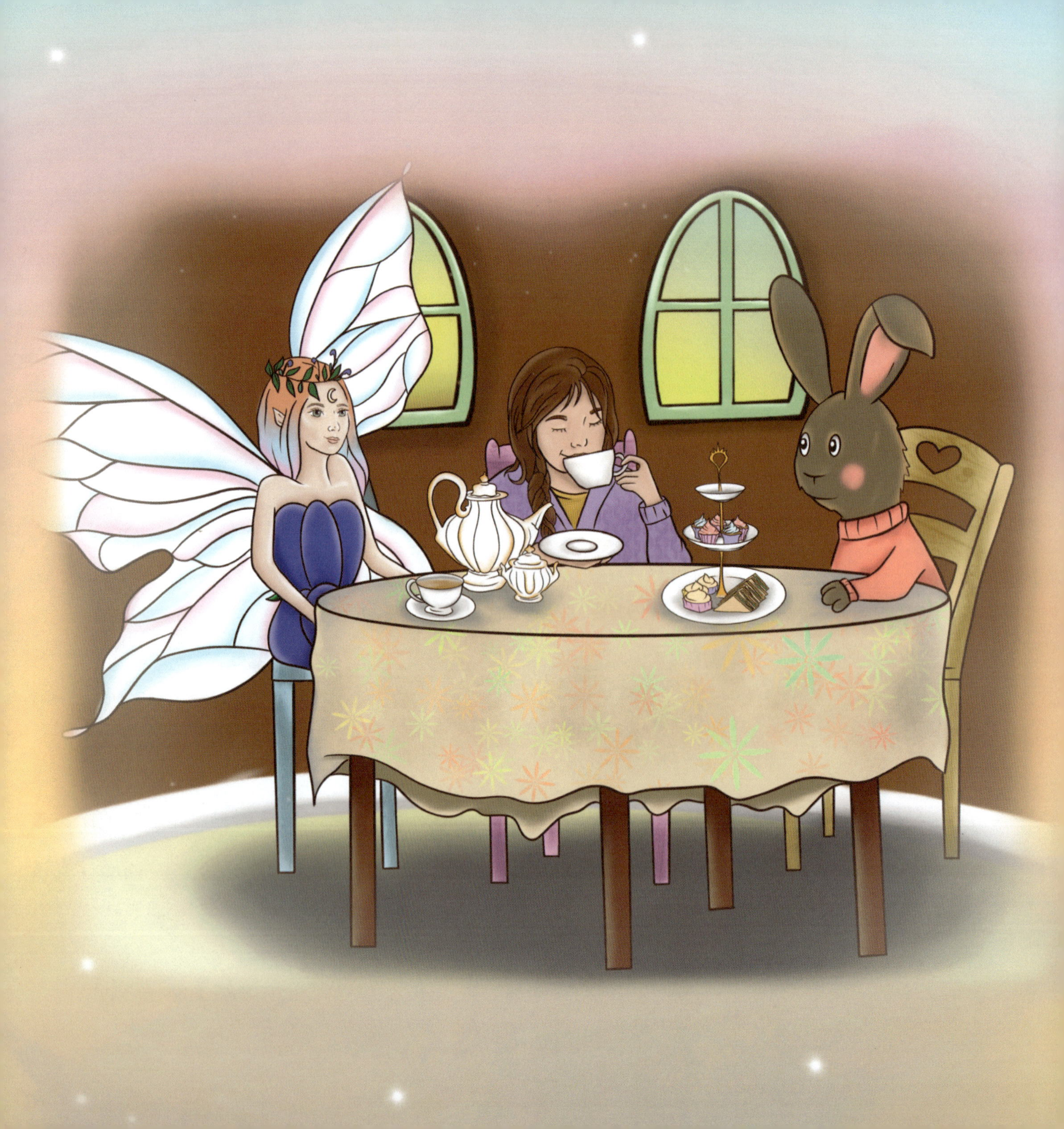

Mrs Quirky pointed Rowena in the right direction. "We will wait for her over there," said Vorriebell. So they all said goodbye and Vorriebell and Rowena waited for Mrs Brown the Rabbit to come home.

"Look there is Mrs Brown now and she is pulling your button along," said Vorriebell. Rowena was so happy when she saw her button.

"Hello vorriebell who is your friend? We don't see humans so small," said Mrs Brown the Rabbit.

"I used my magic to make her small, it was Rowena that made the rain by the Big Wall," said Vorriebell.

"It's been very useful for taking my twins to school they were on time for a change," said Mrs Brown.

"Don't worry," said Rowena "You can keep the button I don't mind about winning the prize for best cardigan now, meeting everyone in the Rainbow Garden is better than any prize."

"That is very kind of you would you like to come in for tea before Vorriebell takes you back to return to normal size and go to school?" said Mrs Brown.

"Yes please." So they all went into her little house by the verge. Rowena could not help noticing she had a table and chairs just like her mums.

After their tea and cake it was time to go back to the wall. Upon leaving, Rowena thanked Mrs Brown for the lovely tea and said she hopes she can come back and meet her twins.

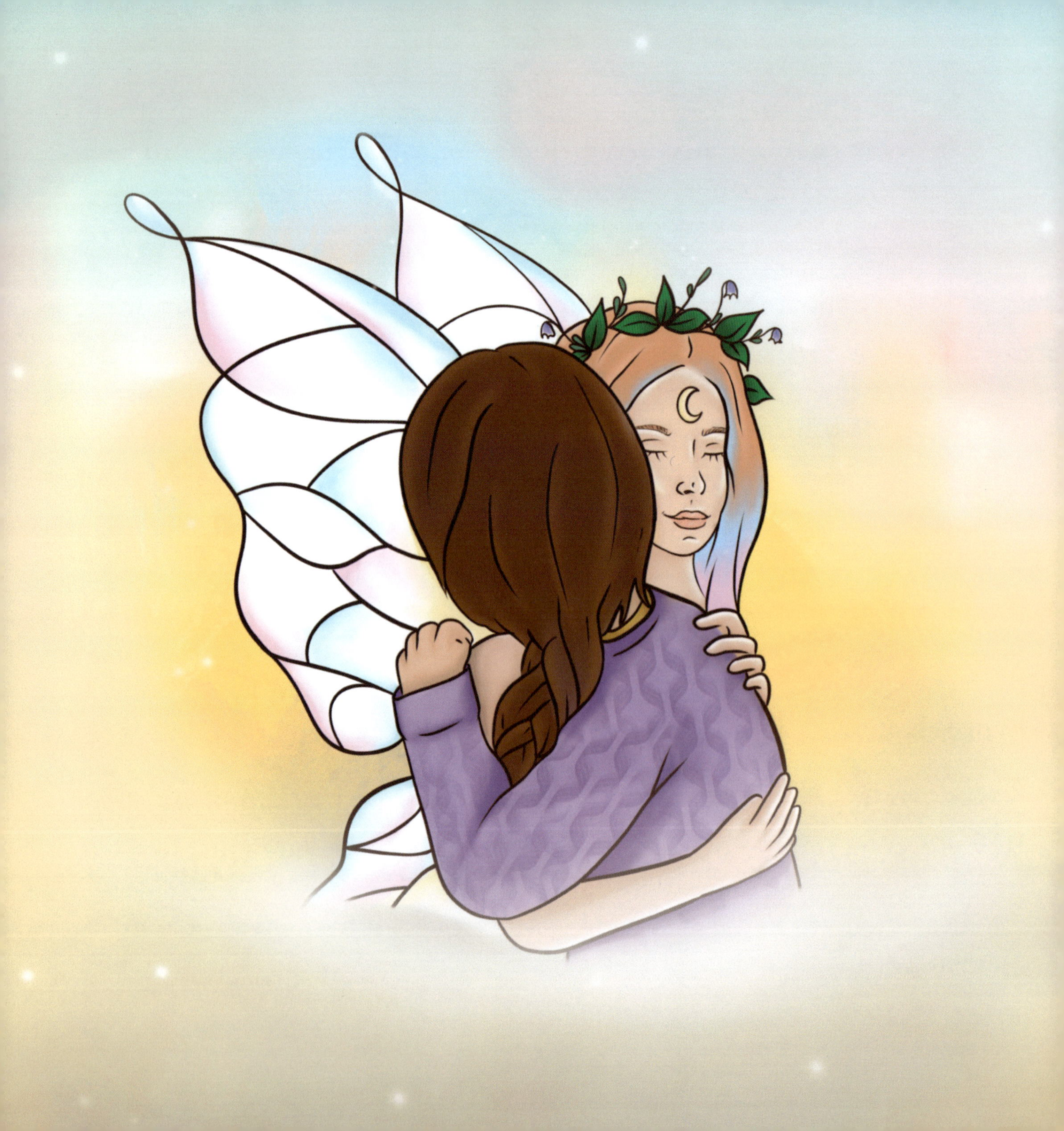

When they returned to the wall Vorriebell gave her a hug and said she was a very special girl then Vorriebell made her tall again.

Rowena climbed the Big Wall then sat for a moment and saw Miss Quirky hanging the washing up, Miss Longlegs bathing in her new web, Mr Brush returning to his home warm and dry and Mr Green happily sitting in his pond with the special flowers making rainbows behind him.

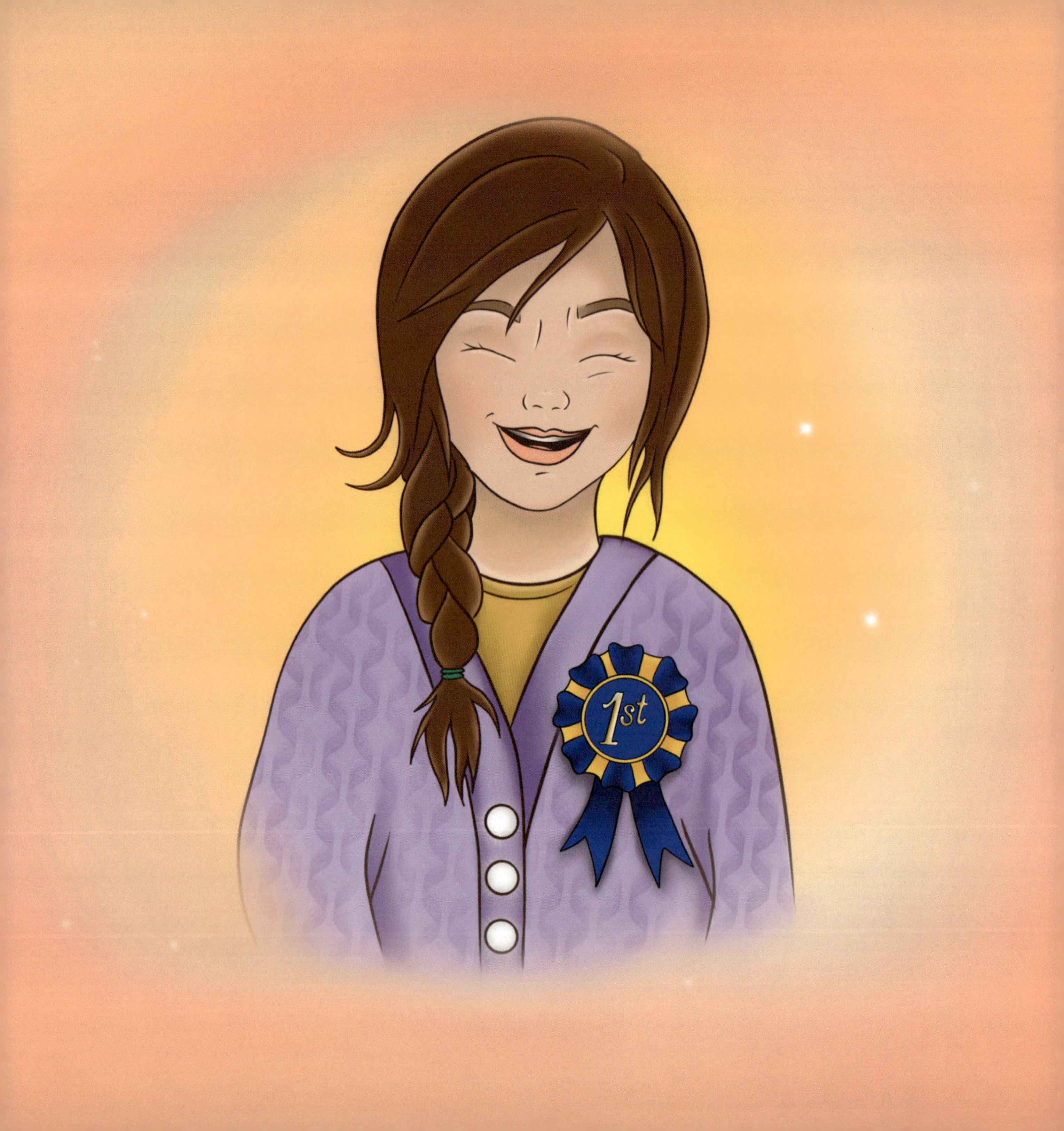
1st

Rowena gave them all a wave and stood up to make her way to school, when she spotted something shining on her cardigan, a sparkling set of new buttons!

She smiled as she knew Vorriebell had made them and used her magic when Rowena was leaving because she promised to keep the garden a secret.

Rowena ended up winning first prize at school and would always be thankful of Vorriebell.

As for The Rainbow Garden The Wise Old Apple Tree was pleased that everyone was happy and all was back to normal… or was it…
Next time see what happens when a naughty mouse makes a visit.

Printed in Great Britain
by Amazon